THE
LOST TRIBES
OF ISRAEL

by

READER HARRIS, KC

THE COVENANT PUBLISHING CO. LTD.

2014

First Edition 1907
Fourth Edition revised 1921
Tenth Edition revised 1941
Eleventh Edition revised 1943
Twelfth Edition revised 2014

ISBN-978-0-85205-101-6

Printed by
THE COVENANT PUBLISHING COMPANY LIMITED
121, Low Etherley, Bishop Auckland,
Co. Durham, DL14 0HA
www.covpub.co.uk

CONTENTS

Cover Picture: River and Mountains in the Caucasus.

Photo, Lafayette.

Reader Harris.

About the Author

Richard Reader Harris, KC (1847-1909), was an eminent English barrister, King's Counsel and Master of the Bench of Gray's Inn, who was also a Methodist minister, founder of the Pentecostal League of Prayer and author of 34 Christian books.

In 1907 he published the first edition of *The Lost Tribes of Israel* which, by its fourth edition in 1921, was recorded as being "25th thousand" in number of copies produced.

As a teenager Reader Harris became a follower of Charles Bradlaugh, the well known London atheist, who (as quoted in this book) stated that God was not a God of truth, because of the failure to keep His promise to Abraham; for not keeping His most solemn promise to establish His Kingdom upon earth through the Patriarch's literal descendants. "Where is that kingdom now?" Bradlaugh said.

For ten years, Harris remained an honest doubter until he met a gifted and cultured lady, Mary Griffin Bristow, whom he married in 1880. They became close friends of the evangelist Oswald Chambers.

Sadly, on 25 March, 1909, Reader Harris suffered a stroke and remained in a coma at his home in London. Without regaining consciousness he died four days later at the age of sixty-one. On 6 April, two thousand people attempted to attend his funeral at West Norwood Cemetery in London. Hundreds of people stood outside.

PREFACE

TO FIRST EDITION

The following is a series of addresses in which I endeavour to give the Scriptural and historical data concerning a subject of consummate interest to all lovers of God's truth.

How I came to deliver these addresses may interest my readers. As an Agnostic years ago I had often heard infidels call attention to the prophecies in the Old Testament concerning Israel which were completely ignored by Christian teachers. When I too became a Christian, I sometimes thought about these prophecies, but for the time satisfied myself with the current explanation that these prophecies referred only to the Church.

A short time ago, however, while studying the history of the Jews, that is to say, the history of portions of the tribes of Judah and Levi, I asked myself, "What about the Ten Tribes, where are their descendants? They must be in existence, they must be an enormous multitude and prophecy must be being fulfilled concerning them."

The following pages are the result of the study which followed. I can now accept a literal interpretation of the Old Testament prophecies concerning the Kingdom of God, while at the same time I can apply them to the present Spiritual Kingdom of this dispensation.

I send forth this little book praying that those who read it may find fresh interest in God's Word.

READER HARRIS

Clapham Common
May, 1907

PREFACE

TO FOURTH EDITION

Thousands of copies of this little volume have, during the last thirteen years, carried a message that has given confidence and inspired praise to God during the anxious days and months and years of the Great War.

The author has passed to his reward, but his words are receiving their confirmation; and since Jerusalem has come into the hands of the British another "fact of stupendous interest" has been added.

M G READER HARRIS

Clapham Common,
June, 1921

TO TWELFTH EDITION

In over 70 years which have passed since the Eleventh Edition of this work the reader will be aware that many changes have occurred to the United Kingdom, the British Empire and Commonwealth and to the Colonies. The State of Israel has been established for 65 years. These changes may at first appear to throw into question some of the conclusions of the author as to the evidence which he presents in support of his arguments.

However, it is important to remember that our understanding of the Scriptures increases as God's plan unfolds. The great changes in our national life and the spiritual declension that we are experiencing now can be seen to have been foretold.

As the author himself says, "Many earnest believers who have been out and out for God on spiritual truth will now be led to consider and study and pray over the literal meaning of these passages."

MICHAEL A CLARK

The Covenant Publishing Company
January, 2014

7

CHAPTER I

ROMANCE OF A GOD-LOVED RACE

The subject of the Lost Tribes of Israel is a study of great interest. Two perplexing questions meet us on the threshold, viz., how is it that so little is known of the ten tribes of Israel, and why has so little enquiry taken place concerning them? This may well be because the devil has succeeded in frustrating any serious research into the matter.

It is remarkable that until the middle of the nineteenth century there was little or no serious enquiry in Protestant countries regarding the fate of the ten tribes; and noteworthy also, that from that period was awakened in some of God's people a spirit of enquiry as to the fate of the ten tribes, with regard to their destiny.

In *Leviticus* 26, in the 18th verse, God says to Israel:

> *"If ye will not hearken unto me, then I will punish you seven times more for your sins."*

Also in the 21st, 24th and 28th verses:

> *"And if ye will not for all this hearken unto me, but walk contrary unto me, then I will walk contrary unto you also in fury; and I, even I, will chastise you seven times for your sins."*

"Seven times" is an interesting period in the Bible. "A time" is generally taken to mean 360 years; "seven times" would mean a period of 2,520 years, which, if calculated from the captivity of Israel, would reach to about the beginning of the nineteenth century. Thus, after the period of "seven times" had run out, there came upon believers in this and in other countries a spirit of enquiry concerning the history and destiny of the ten tribes.

The discovery and acknowledgement of the lost tribes would revolutionise the whole world, give an impetus to Scriptural study, and encourage men in a wonderful degree to believe the promises of God; while on the other hand, if any nation or aggregate of nations could be proved undoubtedly to represent in large measure the ten tribes of Israel, it would inspire them and encourage them to possess their possessions as nothing else could do.

From the "holiness" standpoint and from what I may call that of the "fifth kingdom" (*Daniel* 2), the subject of the history of the lost tribes assumes tremendous importance, and must be of intense interest to every Bible student. The faithfulness of God in regard to every promise, covenant and prophecy, is herein involved. It is a well-known fact that the historian Hume justified his unbelief by what he declared to be the failure of the Bible promises to Israel. I believe that if we study this subject under the light of God's Spirit, resting in the revelation of God's Word, God will give to us, and to others through us, a new interest and confidence in the Bible, a further impetus to religious experience and to prophetic study, and perhaps a clearer apprehension of the political future of the world, and of the signs which foretell the return of our Lord.

JUDAH AND ISRAEL

First and foremost let us understand the difference between the Jews and the lost tribes of Israel; between the kingdom of Judah and the kingdom of Israel. This distinction between the two nations is never lost sight of in the Bible, and until it is understood we cannot follow the Scriptural truth on this subject. The majority of Christian people at the present day have never seen this distinction. They confuse the Jews with the Israelites in various ways. Some in reading of Israel, apply the passage to the Jews, while others think it refers to the Church. Some people apply the curses of the Bible to the Jews, and its promises to the Church. The Bible, however, is perfectly plain. When it speaks of Israel, in ninety-nine cases out of a hundred the ten tribes are meant. There are some few passages where the word "Israel" undoubtedly refers, as it did originally, to the twelve tribes of Israel; but, generally speaking, there is a marked and definite distinction between Judah and Israel, and unless we realise that distinction we cannot understand the prophecies concerning this wonderful people.

That the missing tribes exist no serious person can doubt. If, under persecution such as the world has never before seen, after massacre upon massacre, torture upon torture, the remnant of part of the tribes of Judah, Levi and Benjamin, can have multiplied until they reach something like fourteen millions of people, what must be the number today of the ten tribes? Ten tribes equally virile; ten tribes of the same stock; ten tribes that have lived their lives and spread their race without persecution, massacre and torture! What a multitude must they now have become! Where are they?

HISTORY OF ISRAEL

Let us begin with their earliest history. God chose Abraham, and made an unconditional covenant with his lineal seed (*Genesis* 22:15-18). That covenant was repeated by God to Jacob when He called him Israel, as you will see in *Genesis* 35:11:

> *"God said unto him, I am God Almighty. Be fruitful and multiply. A nation and a company of nations shall be of thee, and kings shall come out of thy loins."*

Jacob before his death blessed the sons of Joseph, Ephraim and Manasseh, giving the birthright to Ephraim, although Ephraim was not the elder of the two. If you will look at *Genesis* 48, you will see that the blessing which ought to have been Reuben's was taken from him because of his sin and given to Ephraim. Judah received the emblem of the Lion, and obtained the promises of kingship, and that from him should spring the Messiah. Moses before his death blessed the sons of Joseph,

Ephraim and Manasseh, and gave to them the emblem of the Unicorn (*Deuteronomy* 33:17). It is remarkable that so far back as the days of Moses the emblems of the Lion and the Unicorn pertained to Judah and Ephraim.

The distinction between the two nations of Judah and Israel began before their final separation under Jeroboam and Rehoboam. You will find in II *Samuel* 2, that David was anointed king over Judah only, while Ishbosheth, Saul's son, was made king over all Israel, this severance continuing for seven and a half years. Israel was then annexed to Judah under King David (II *Samuel* 5:1), but the two kingdoms of Judah and Israel were finally separated immediately after the death of Solomon, and from that time to the present Judah and Israel have remained absolutely distinct. They were carried into captivity separately, at different times and by different nations, for Israel was taken into captivity by the Assyrians 721 BC (II *Kings* 17:6), while Judah was carried into captivity by the Babylonians 588 BC (II *Kings* 25:21). A portion of Judah was permitted to return after seventy years, as had been predicted (*Ezra* 2:1), but Israel never returned, nor was there any prediction that they should return till the final glorious restoration.

In 721 BC the ten tribes of Israel drop out of sacred history, and there is no further reference made to them in the historical part of the Bible, but the prophetical portions supply the sequel, for in these Scriptural prophecies the whole future of the people of Israel is chronicled. Apart from the sacred books we find the last historical record of the ten tribes is given by the great Jewish historian Josephus, writing from Rome, in AD 70: Ant. xi, 2:

> "The entire body of the ten tribes are still beyond the river Euphrates, an immense multitude not to be estimated by numbers."

We see, therefore, that the kingdom of Judah and the kingdom of Israel, ever since the day of Solomon, have been absolutely distinct. What the future of Israel was to be, actually has been, and may be, will form the subject of my next chapter.

I propose now to give a short outline of the history of the kingdom of *Judah*, for to understand the history of the ten tribes we must study the history of Judah, Levi and Benjamin.

HISTORY OF JUDAH

After the death of Solomon, his son Rehoboam became king of the tribes of Judah and Benjamin, which were afterwards joined by the tribe of Levi. Levi first united with Israel, but when Jeroboam, the son of Nebat, "who made Israel to sin," raised the golden calves and called upon the Israelites to worship them, the tribe of Levi refused to perform the religious ceremonies, and were in consequence banished by this king. The Levites then joined Rehoboam, thus uniting themselves with the tribes of Judah and Benjamin. Jeroboam became king of the ten tribes now known as Israel, which, after 250 years of unexampled wickedness, were carried captive into Assyria in 721 BC, their country being peopled by Assyrians.

Judah, Levi and Benjamin were carried away captive to Babylon about 588 BC. The book of *Daniel* gives the story of their sojourn there. After seventy years Cyrus the Persian set them at liberty, and gave them permission to return to Jerusalem. On their return they rebuilt Jerusalem and the temple, re-instituted the temple services, and became known to the world as Jews. This name was probably derived from, or cognate with, the names of Judah and Jerusalem, and from that time the three tribes of Judah, Levi and Benjamin were called Jews.

For several centuries they maintained what may be called a revived national existence, but they suffered much from their enemies, and were more or less under the control of the Persians, followed by that of the Greeks and Egyptians, and finally by the dominion of the Romans. When the Messiah came, the Jews, or rather the tribes of Judah and Levi, as was predicted, put Him to death, saying *"His blood be on us and on our children"* (*Matthew* 27:25), which saying has been fulfilled in terrible measure. The tribe of Benjamin seems to have taken no part in putting our Lord to death.

HISTORY OF BENJAMIN

The story of this tribe is of special interest. In the prophecies of the Old Testament, Benjamin is generally reckoned among the ten tribes. God only promised Solomon that his son should have one tribe to follow him. At the disruption, however, Benjamin joined Judah, and went into and returned from captivity with Judah and Levi; but it is an historical fact that the tribe of Benjamin was free from the awful sin of the crucifixion of the Son of God. Nearly all the Apostles, including Paul, belonged to the tribe of Benjamin. At the destruction of Jerusalem in AD 70 the tribe of Benjamin had very largely become Christian, and, according to Josephus, every one of its members escaped destruction. The tribe of Benjamin eventually fled from Judaea and joined the ten tribes of Israel in Asia Minor *beyond the River Euphrates*, and with them from that time has rested the fulfilment of biblical prophecy.

MODERN HISTORY OF THE JEWS

The subsequent history of the Jews, the tribes of Judah and Levi, is well known, so I will merely call your attention to some of the salient points. The Romans under Titus, after a terrible struggle of nearly five years, destroyed Jerusalem in AD 70. A million Jews perished and multitudes were sold unto slavery. Sixty years after Hadrian slaughtered 580,000 Jews and sent all the others he could capture into slavery. The remainder took refuge in other lands. From the reign of Hadrian to that of Constantine the Jews who had settled in the Roman Empire prospered. We find them very active allies of the heathen against the early Christians, and they were in a great many cases the instigators of persecution, for they still hated Christ and persecuted His followers. It is said that Jews carried the faggots to the stake at the martyrdom of the venerable Polycarp.

With the conversion of the Emperor Constantine to Christianity, however, the position of the Jews was altered. They now became in their turn a persecuted people, and for hundreds of years suffered almost indescribable persecution. At last they took refuge in Spain, and there by their extraordinary ability to gain money they amassed enormous fortunes, becoming large landowners, and eventually holding the purse-strings of the nation. Persecution then broke out. They were massacred, tortured by the Inquisition, or driven from the country, leaving everything behind them. The same story was repeated throughout Europe at the time of the Crusades. We associate the Crusades with Peter the Hermit's preaching of that wonderful sermon "Deus Vult," "God wills it"—namely, the deliverance of the Holy Sepulchre from the Saracen yoke—but, in actual fact, the Crusades are more to be remembered by the terrible massacre of the Jews throughout Europe than by any victories gained over the Saracens. Every army marching through Europe to the Holy Land massacred the Jews on its way, and for 200 years, while the Crusading armies were marching or counter-marching, the Jews suffered persecution of a terrible kind, which continued all through the Middle Ages and in a measure to the present day.

We ourselves have been shocked by the recent repeated massacres of the Jews in Russia. A Jew in Russia at the present period has all kinds of limitations placed upon him. He may only educate a portion of his family. He is not allowed to enter any of the professions. His tenure of property is different from that of anybody else, and he is denied the right to hold land. Every country, except Great Britain and the United States, is all but impossible to the Jew. Ever since the Jews' rejection of Jesus Christ their lot has been one of nothing but desolation, degradation and misery. To-day they number in all, perhaps, twelve or fourteen millions; a scattered people, without land and without government, without metropolis and without temple; a race, in faith and in religious observance, exactly fulfilling God's prophecy concerning them; an object-lesson to all humanity; an object-lesson of the destiny of those who reject the Son of God.

Prophecy, which has been fulfilled to the very letter in regard to the Jew, has, I believe, also been fulfilled to the very letter in regard to Israel. The ten tribes of Israel have another history, which we will consider in the following chapters.[1]

---

[1] This was written before the Jew had a home promised him in Palestine by the British (10th Edition).

CHAPTER II

THE LOST TRIBES—WHERE ARE THEY?

In the previous chapter we studied the difference between Judah and Israel. (That distinction runs through the Bible and is never lost sight of.) We saw that ever since the men of Judah rejected Jesus Christ their lot has been desolation, degradation and misery. But Israel has another story, and I begin the study of the history of the so-called lost tribes of Israel with this declaration: The lost tribes, the descendants of the kingdom of Israel, are certainly in existence to-day. But where? That is the question, and what a wonderful question it is! The discovery of a continent is a great discovery, and Columbus will be celebrated throughout all time as the discoverer of a continent. The discovery of a new star, a new world, is a great discovery. But I venture to think that the discovery of the kingdom of Israel, of the descendants of those ten tribes, would have a greater effect upon the kingdom of God and the hearts and lives of men than even the discovery of a new continent or of a new world.

The descendants of the tribes of Israel certainly exist; the question is, Where? The Jews we know, but where is Israel? Some people assert that God has cut Israel out of His divine programme, and in consequence Israel has become extinct as a nation. In refutation of such a statement let us turn to *Jeremiah* 31:35, 36:

> *"Thus saith the Lord, which giveth the sun for a light by day, and the ordinances of the moon and of the stars for a light by night, which divideth* [which stilleth] *the sea when the waves thereof roar: The Lord of Hosts is his name: If those ordinances* [that is, the sun, moon and stars] *depart from before me, saith the Lord, then the seed of Israel also shall cease from being a nation before me for ever."*

This passage distinctly declares that while sun and moon and stars exist the nation of Israel will remain before God.

A GREAT QUESTION

Where are the ten tribes? Where is the nation of Israel? Which nation on earth to-day represents them? How can this be discovered? I have learned that if we really want to know about God's people, the Bible is the Book in which to look; let us, therefore, go to the Bible for the history of God's chosen people Israel. Unless God's promises have failed, Israel must be in existence to-day.

We shall find that the Bible declares that Israel exists as a multitudinous nation, bearing certain marks, inheriting certain blessings, doing certain things for which it was created, and which it was, and is, its special mission and destiny to perform. The ten tribes are in existence somewhere, and the quest is not so difficult as it at first appears, for although secular history is apparently dumb concerning these tribes—a remarkable fact in itself—Bible prophecy is abundant in descriptive allusion to Israel; and we shall find from the study of biblical prophecy where the kingdom of Israel is to-day. To the Scriptures then let us turn, and may the Spirit of Truth light up the Word to us.

JUDAH AND ISRAEL

Let me first show you some points of difference between the prophecies concerning Judah and those concerning Israel. Out of Judah we read that there was to come one seed only, namely, the Messiah (I *Chronicles* 5:2). Out of Israel, on the other hand, it is prophesied that a numerous seed should spring (*Genesis* 48:16), through whom the blessings obtained by Christ would be spread abroad (*Isaiah* 66:19), Judah is to be few in number (*Jeremiah* 15:7; *Ezekiel* 12:16); but Israel is to be as the sand on the sea-shore (*Hosea* 1:10). Judah's house is to be left desolate (*Matthew* 23:38); while Israel's seed is by adoption to become sons of the living God (*Hosea* 1 and 2). Judah is to be separate from the nations, its people exposed to reproach and shame (*Jeremiah* 24:9), and their countenances witnessing against them (*Isaiah* 3:9). Israel, lost to view among the Gentiles (*Isaiah* 54:3; *Hosea* 7:8), is to be sought out and discovered as being the sons of the living God (*Hosea* 1:10; *Ezekiel* 37:12).

OLD TESTAMENT PROPHECIES

Let us now turn to some prophecies concerning Israel in the Old Testament.

> *"Sing with gladness for Jacob, and shout among the chief of the nations; publish ye, praise ye, and say, O Lord, save thy people, the remnant of Israel"* (*Jeremiah* 31:7).

This cannot refer to the Jews, who have never formed a nation since their captivity.

Israel, after a period of punishment for their sins, were to be wanderers among the nations, but after that time they were to be gathered from among the Gentiles into a place of safety.

> *"Lo, I will command, and I will cause to move to and fro the house of Israel among all nations"* (*Amos* 9:9 R.V.).

> *"Hear the word of the Lord, O ye nations, and declare it in the isles afar off, and say, He that scattered Israel will gather him, and keep him as a shepherd doth his flock"* (*Jeremiah* 31:10).

Israel's population shall increase as a fruitful bough whose branches shall run over the wall.

> *"Joseph is a fruitful bough, even a fruitful bough by a well; whose branches run over the wall"* (*Genesis* 49:22).

Israel is to colonise the desolate heritages and cause the deserts to blossom as the rose.

*"He shall cause them that come of Jacob to take root;
Israel shall blossom and bud, and fill the face of the world
with fruit"* (*Isaiah* 27:6).

Israel is to develop into a company of nations.

*"And God said unto him, I am God Almighty: be
fruitful and multiply. A nation and a company of nations
shall be of thee, and kings shall come out of thy loins"*
(*Genesis* 35:11).

Israel is to possess the gate of his enemies.

*"In blessing I will bless thee, and in multiplying I will
multiply thy seed as the stars of the heaven, and as the sand
which is upon the sea shore; and thy seed shall possess the
gate of his enemies"* (*Genesis* 22:17).

Israel's emblem is the unicorn.

*"His horns are like the horns of unicorns; with them he
shall push the people together to the ends of the earth: and
they are the ten thousands of Ephraim, and they are the
thousands of Manasseh"* (*Deuteronomy* 33:17).

Israel is to lend to many nations and borrow from none.

*"Thou shalt lend unto many nations, and thou shalt not
borrow"* (*Deuteronomy* 28:12).

Unlike Judah, Israel is to be known upon earth by another
name.

*"And ye shall leave your name ... for the Lord God
shall ... call his servants by another name"* (*Isaiah* 65:15).

Israel shall be known in history as a nation which
suppresses slavery and tyranny.

"Is not this the fast that I have chosen? to loose the bands of wickedness, to undo the heavy burdens, and to let the oppressed go free, and that ye break every yoke?" (*Isaiah* 58:6).

Israel is to be a maritime people.

"I will set his hand also in the sea, and his right hand in the rivers" (*Psalm* 89:25; *Zechariah* 9:10).

Israel is to be a conquering power, with the lion as one of its emblems.

"And the remnant of Jacob shall be among the Gentiles in the midst of many people as a lion among the beasts of the forest, as a young lion among the flocks of sheep: who, if he go through, both treadeth down, and teareth in pieces, and none can deliver" (*Micah* 5:8).

Israel is to rule over many nations and to be ruled by none.

"Thou shalt reign over many nations, but they shall not reign over thee" (*Deuteronomy* 15:6).

Israel is to have a separate political existence; and also to become a great people.

"His [Ephraim's] *seed shall become a multitude of nations"* (*Genesis* 48:19).

Lastly, Israel is to become heir of the world.

"For the promise that he should be the heir of the world was not to Abraham, or to his seed, through the law, but through the righteousness of faith" (*Romans* 4:13).

These Scriptural prophecies about Israel have a plain literal meaning as well as a spiritual meaning. In the past many of us have taken these passages and dealt with them from a purely spiritual standpoint, and in so doing we have been greatly blessed by God. But a distinct prophecy must, of course, have a literal signification as well as a spiritual one, and the prophecies concerning Israel must have a literal as well as a spiritual fulfilment, and are just as sure as those concerning Judah. The prophecies about Israel, indeed, are far more numerous than those about Judah.

NEW TESTAMENT PROPHECIES

Let us now turn to the New Testament. It is perfectly clear that Israel, who had been dispersed for more than 700 years, was much in our Lord's mind during His three years' ministry upon earth, for many were the references to Israel made by Him. As an example, let us turn to the commission He gave to the twelve apostles in *Matthew* 10:5, 6:

> *"These twelve Jesus sent forth, and commanded them, saying, Go not into the way of the Gentiles, and into any city of the Samaritans enter ye not: But go rather to the lost sheep of the house of Israel."*

These apostles were not to go to the Gentiles nor to the Samaritans—who were the descendants of usurpers of Israel— "But to the lost sheep of the house of Israel," and they obeyed this command as far as was then possible. The only tribe that they could reach which had any connection with Israel was Benjamin, and Benjamin as a tribe was won to allegiance to the Lord Jesus Christ. Benjamin had gone into captivity with Judah, and had come back with Judah, but, in the prophecies of God, Benjamin had been always associated with the ten tribes of Israel. It is a remarkable fact that the majority of our Lord's disciples at the time of His earthly ministry were connected with the tribe of Benjamin.[2] It is also of interest that when Jerusalem was afterwards besieged by the Romans under Titus, the

---

[2] Judas Iscariot ... was perhaps the only Jew in the Apostolic band. – Farrar's *Life of Christ*, p.117 (10th Edition).

members of what had become the Christian tribe of Benjamin escaped.

Christ Himself declared in *Matthew* 15:24, this was His Own mission.

"He answered and said, I am not sent but unto the lost sheep of the house of Israel."

Again, our Lord says in *Matthew* 21:43:

"Therefore say I unto you [He was speaking to the Jews], *The kingdom of God shall be taken from you and given to a nation* [the Jews had long since ceased to be a nation] *bringing forth the fruits thereof."*

The Jews themselves evidently so understood His statement for in *John* 7:35 we read:

"Then said the Jews among themselves, Whither will He go, that we shall not find Him? Will He go unto the dispersed among the Gentiles, and teach the Gentiles?"

So the Jews quite understood our Lord to refer to Israel.

Israel was evidently in the minds of the apostles themselves. On the day of the ascension they asked Him:

"Lord, wilt thou at this time restore again the kingdom to Israel?" (*Acts* 1:6).

A restoration of the kingdom of Israel with the kingdom of Judah had been promised. The apostles did not confuse the kingdom of Israel with that of Judah, for they said: "Wilt Thou at this time restore the kingdom to Israel?" St. Paul devotes thirty-six verses in *Romans* 11 to prove that God has not cast away His people, but that "blindness in part has happened unto Israel until the fulness of the nations be come in," so that all Israel shall be saved. The kingdom of stone had to wait for the four previous ones referred to in Nebuchadnezzar's vision. The epistle of *James* was written in AD 60 "to the twelve tribes scattered abroad." By that time some of the Jews were dispersed as well. Both Peter's epistles were written especially to those who were scattered abroad throughout Pontus, Galatia, Cappadocia, Asia, and Bithynia.

Lastly, the final word must be that of our Lord. In *Acts* 1:7, 8, Christ said:

> *"It is not for you to know the times or the seasons, which the Father hath put in His own power. But ye shall receive power, after that the Holy Ghost is come upon you; and ye shall be witnesses unto me both in Jerusalem, and in all Judaea, and in Samaria, and unto the uttermost part of the earth."*

i.e. "to the regions beyond," an expression that was fully understood to mean the dispersed among the Gentiles. To paraphrase our Lord's words in this passage: "The restoration of Israel is an important matter, but at the moment there is something more important, which is, that there is a blessing for you to claim, and a work for you to accomplish, and power shall be given from on high that shall enable you to accomplish it, which is the mighty power of the Holy Ghost. You must be filled with the Holy Ghost—that is the chief need; you are 'to be witnesses to Me in Jerusalem, in all Judaea, in Samaria, and unto the uttermost part of the earth.'" And that is our commission to-day.

A WITNESSING KINGDOM

Although it is very interesting and important that we Christians should read the Bible and understand its meaning, not merely in its purely spiritual aspect but also in its plain literal meaning, it is more important still that we should be "filled unto all the fulness of God." It is only as we are filled with the Holy

Ghost that we can understand God's Word or that we can be witnesses unto Jesus Christ either at home or abroad.

I believe that these "times and seasons" which were not ripe on the day of ascension, are now becoming ripe. Spiritual life and blessing is, I believe, to be reinforced by actual, visible, literal results, and probably the whole is rapidly nearing a crisis. "The times and seasons" are in God's hands, "*but* ye shall receive power after that the Holy Ghost is come upon you, and ye shall be witnesses unto Me in Jerusalem, in all Judaea, in Samaria, and unto the uttermost part of the earth." Let us remember that their witness was not a witness primarily concerning the Jew or the Israelite, but concerning the Lord Jesus Christ and His uttermost salvation. May God give us the grace and power that we may shine for Him where He has placed us, that we may be His witnesses in the homes where He has put us, in the churches where we worship, in the places where we labour, in the streets where we walk, and in the lives which we live for His glory.

It is well to know this Book, to revel in its wondrous truth, to feed our souls on the Word of God. But God wants us not merely to know wonderful things, but that we should ourselves be living epistles, read of all men; men and women who are witnesses unto Jesus Christ. Therefore as we study this great subject, and, like those men and women of old, ask: "Wilt Thou restore the kingdom to Israel?"—let us learn Christ's answer: There is first something for us to be, and then for us to do, the being and the doing of which shall hasten the accomplishment of all things, including the return of our Lord and the restoration of Israel.

CHAPTER III

SCRIPTURAL AND HISTORICAL EVIDENCES

In the first chapter we studied the difference between the house of Judah and the house of Israel. In the second we dealt with the prophecies concerning the kingdom of Judah and the kingdom of Israel.

I will now state some of the chief reasons which have led many earnest Christians to believe that the British Empire and the house of Israel are identical. Let us study the Scripture and consider the historical facts that have influenced some of the deepest thinkers, some of God's most honoured servants, in coming to this conclusion.

THE GENERAL ARGUMENT

The Bible predicts the rise and fall of the most important nations of the earth, from the time of Nebuchadnezzar to the end of the age. The interpretation of the prophet Daniel of Nebuchadnezzar's dream of the image with the head of gold and so on, has been generally accepted by Christendom as teaching the history of the world kingdoms from then to the end of the age—the Babylonian kingdom, the Medo-Persian kingdom, the Grecian kingdom, and the Roman Empire, followed by the Stone kingdom. As the Bible has given us this revelation, I ask you—Is it likely that the nation which God chose for Himself has been wiped out completely? Is it likely that in this inspired prophecy concerning the great kingdoms of this world, the British Empire, far greater than any other, the greatest and most favoured empire the world has ever known, should be omitted? Are we to believe that this great, wealthy, and highly favoured empire is not referred to in this Book of inspired prophecy? Is it not likely that the fifth kingdom in Daniel's prophecy, the Stone kingdom, may refer to Israel and to the kingdom that is represented by Great Britain to-day?

Let us, therefore, as the Spirit shall guide us, compare what the Bible declares Israel should be with what Great Britain is today. We may find that the purpose of God has been fulfilled, and the mantle of Israel has fallen upon the British or Anglo-Saxon race.

THE SCRIPTURAL EVIDENCES

(1).   Israel is to become a multitudinous race of immense power. God, in speaking to Abram, says:

"I will make thy seed as the dust of the earth, so that if a man can number the dust of the earth then shall thy seed also be numbered" (*Genesis* 13:16).

"And God brought him forth abroad, and said, Look now toward Heaven, and tell the stars, if thou be able to number them: and he said unto him, So shall thy seed be" (*Genesis* 15:5).

And again, after his name became Abraham:

"In blessing I will bless thee, and in multiplying I will multiply thy seed as the stars of the heaven, and as the sand which is upon the sea shore: and thy seed shall possess the gate of his enemies; And in thy seed shall all the nations of the earth be blessed; because thou hast obeyed my voice" (*Genesis* 22:17, 18).

Note that these are unconditional promises which God is bound to fulfil.

Let us now consider existing facts concerning the British race. In the year AD 1700 the British race numbered only a few millions; in 1800 about 25 millions; whereas in 1900 they numbered 130 millions. In another century the British race will probably be more numerous than all the other nations of the earth put together, truly "a multitude as the stars of heaven." I will now give you the opinions of some eminent men who have spoken on this subject, men who were not necessarily in sympathy with what is known as the British-Israel teaching. An old personal friend of my own, Admiral Sir John Colomb, KCMG, who has recently retired from the House of Commons, said in 1900:

"The British Empire literally encircles the earth. It comprises more than nine millions of square miles of the earth's surface, one-fifth part of the whole habitable globe, the largest empire of either ancient or modern times."

Sir Charles Dilke in the same year said:

"The British Empire has an area of, roughly speaking, three Europes; lying in all latitudes and producing every requirement of life and trade, in addition to which, it has half the sea-borne commerce of the world."

The Times newspaper in the same year bears the same testimony. In a leading article on this subject we read:

"The British are gradually filling continents, fringing oceans, and making the whole world their home. We are, in fact, peopling the greater portion of the globe."

The late Lord Beaconsfield, who was himself a Jew, said of the British race:

"History will recognise the destiny of the British race, but history will never record its decline or fall. History will say, 'This is *the* great, the understanding people.'"

Sir Howard Vincent in 1900 said:[3]
"Think of the British Empire! Let us get an idea of its immensity. Fifty-two times the size of Germany, and seven times its population; 53 times the size of France, and nine

[3] Note the date of these remarks. Since then things have progressed immensely – Ed. (10th Edition).

times its population; 3 ½ times the size of the United States, and 4 ½ times its population. The British Empire has now a population of over 350 millions of people, with an annual revenue of 300 millions of pounds sterling, with an annual trade amounting to 1,200 million pounds sterling, carried in 40,000 British ships of an aggregate burden of 10 million tons."

These figures give us an idea of the immensity of the British Empire.

FURTHER EVIDENCES

(2).   Israel is to be a blessing to the whole world.

"This people have I formed for myself: they shall show forth my praise" (*Isaiah* 43:21).

"The remnant of Jacob shall be in the midst of many people as a dew from the Lord, as the shower upon the grass" (*Micah* 5:7).

Great Britain alone of all the nations can be taken to fulfil this prophecy. *The Times* newspaper in 1900 said:

"There is not a region in the world in which the British race is not striving to do good. The money contributed in one year for missionary work in the British Isles is twelve times the contributions of all the other nations of the earth put together."

"However we may explain it, Europe leaves to Britain the main portion of the work of international beneficence. It is to England that every nation in turn appeals in its hour of tribulation with a confident assurance that the appeal will be answered."

"It is not so with other nations. Indeed Britain has learned to accept the task of administering to the world's needs at Britain's own cost."

An eminent Churchman has said:

> "God is training the Anglo-Saxon race to fulfil the Divine admonition. This Gospel of the kingdom shall be preached in all the world for a witness unto all nations."

A great Nonconformist has said:

> "It is almost impossible to get out of sight of our race. The Cross of the Lord Jesus Christ is the standard and the starting point of a mighty company of brave and noble men and women, who go into all the world to preach the gospel to every creature."

This is not boasting; these are facts which very many people are satisfied are in fulfilment of Divine prophecy. God gave a commission to Israel in *Isaiah* 58:6, to

> *"Loose the bands of wickedness, to undo the heavy burdens and to let the oppressed go free, and that ye break every yoke."*

What other nation but Britain has ever fulfilled that prophecy? In 1807 Great Britain abolished the slave trade in every part of her dominions, and paid twenty millions of pounds sterling in compensation. Fifty years later the United States freed her slaves, at the cost of a civil war. Wherever possible Great Britain has intervened in other countries, and wherever her influence has been paramount, slavery has been abolished.

(3).   Israel is to be an invincible nation.

> *"No weapon that is formed against thee shall prosper"* (*Isaiah* 54:17).

> *"Fear thou not* [Israel], *for I am with thee; be not dismayed: for I am thy God: I will strengthen thee; yea, I will help thee; yea, I will uphold thee"* (*Isaiah* 41:10).

We have been in the habit of taking such a passage and spiritualising it, and saying that it refers to the Church, or to individuals. So it does, thank God; and in taking the literal meaning of these words, we are not lessening their spiritual meaning. But when God Almighty writes a sentence He will fulfil the literal meaning of those words as well as their spiritual meaning; so I venture to think that these words have, perhaps, a fuller and more literal meaning than we have hitherto attributed to them.

The passages from *Isaiah* just quoted have been fulfilled. Can any other nation on the face of the earth claim that she has been uniformly victorious on land and on sea? The same God who gave victory to Israel in the Red Sea gave victory to Britain against the Spanish Armada and at the battle of Waterloo. In the Prayer Book, in the liturgy of the Church of England, we daily confess:

"It is God alone who fighteth for us."

Is there any other nation possessing in its national ritual such a declaration as this?

(4). Israel is to hold the gate of her enemies.

"Thy seed shall possess the gate of her enemies" (*Genesis* 22:17 and 24:60).

Great Britain holds the sea: This includes Gibraltar, which opens Spain to our arms and the Mediterranean to our navies; Malta, a place of arms, from which this country could easily invade half-a-dozen European countries; Singapore, the gate of the East; Malacca, Hong Kong, Cyprus, Aden, the Khyber Pass; and, in addition, stretching right across the Atlantic and Pacific Oceans, a string of 45 coaling stations for British ships. Great Britain holds the gate of her enemies in a very remarkable degree.

(5).   Israel is to be a great money-lending nation.

"Thou shalt lend unto many nations, and thou shalt not borrow" (Deuteronomy 28:12).

This prophecy is fulfilled by no other nation but Great Britain. Every other nation has borrowed, and that from Great Britain, but she has borrowed of none. Great Britain receives yearly 50 or 60 millions of pounds sterling in interest upon her loans to other nations.

There are many other remarkable prophecies about Israel which are fulfilled by the British race, but there is yet one more remarkable than any I have given you, and which is also of a specially sacred character.

The observance of a Sabbath has been given by God as a sign which shall mark Israel for ever.

"The children of Israel shall keep the Sabbath, to observe the Sabbath throughout their generations for a perpetual covenant; It is a sign between me and the children of Israel for ever" (Exodus 31:16, 17).

The British Nation and United States alone of the nations on earth possess this sign. Dr Ryle, the late Bishop of Liverpool, said:

"I assert without hesitation that the only countries on the face of the globe in which you will find a true observance of the Sabbath are Great Britain and her colonies."

He was right. Compare other countries, and the way they spend the Sabbath! There may be in some a semblance of worship in the morning, but the rest of the day is given up to military reviews, races, theatres, balls, and bull-fights. No other nation but Great Britain and United State can possibly be said to fulfil this sign. Voltaire, the arch-infidel, a man of extraordinary intellectual power, said:

"Whether Englishmen know it or not, it is the English Sunday which makes England what England is."

Some of you may have visited the last Paris Exhibition. One thing was observed by everybody who went there, that while all the other sections of the Exhibition were open and at work on Sunday—all the machinery at work, all the stalls open—the British department and the United States department were completely closed. Why is it, therefore, that of all the nations, Great Britain and her sixty colonies and the United States of America alone observe the Christian Sabbath? God answers that question in these words:

"It is a sign between me and the children of Israel for ever."

Such then are the Scriptures that appear to me to furnish strong evidence in favour of the contention of those who believe that in the Anglo-Saxon race God possesses to-day the descendants of the house of Israel. If this be true, it adds tremendously to our responsibilities, and opens before us in a way that no human tongue can describe, spiritual possibilities, temporal possibilities, national possibilities, and universal possibilities.

Let none of us, however, be so taken up with the literal fulfilment of prophecy that we forget the spiritual application of it. For this reason it is extremely important that those who study this subject should be filled with the Spirit of wisdom and revelation in the full knowledge of the Lord Jesus Christ, and should themselves be in the full experience of spiritual blessing.

Let us, therefore, claim God's Spirit, and as we learn day by day to see more evidences of the fulfilment of these prophecies, may God possess in us individually, and in the Pentecostal League collectively, and in the thousands of others who are in sympathy with us, a body of men and women yielded to Him in heart, and in life, learning His will, proclaiming His truth, and glorifying His name.

CHAPTER IV

EPHRAIM AND MANASSEH

L et us now study the history of Ephraim and Manasseh. I will take for a text some words in *Jeremiah* 31:9: "Ephraim is my firstborn." These words were spoken by the prophet Jeremiah concerning Israel more than 100 years after Israel had gone into captivity. The whole of this 31st chapter of *Jeremiah* is understood to be of special significance when it is remembered that it was written long after the captivity of the house of Israel, and contains promise after promise inspired by God concerning His people Israel.

The story of Ephraim and Manasseh is very interesting. The patriarch Jacob was the inheritor of the promises made to Abraham, which promises included five things: First, an everlasting covenant (*Genesis* 17:7); second, the possession of the land of Canaan (*Genesis* 17:8); third, a multitude of seed (*Genesis* 17:2); fourth, to be the father of many nations (*Genesis* 17:5); fifth that his seed was to be a source of blessing to the whole world (*Genesis* 22:18). Such were the promises made to Abraham and inherited by Jacob. The possession of the birthright which Esau had despised and which Jacob had coveted, was confirmed to the letter by God at Bethel, and again at Peniel, when he obtained the name of Israel as a prince with God, and, lastly, at Padan-aram. We see therefore that Jacob received the promises made to Abraham. Jacob had twelve sons, whom before his death he blessed. Reuben, the eldest, was deprived of his birthright—the birthright of the eldest son— because of his sin, and as a consequence it was given to Joseph (I *Chronicles* 5:2), and in turn was settled on his two sons, Ephraim and Manasseh.

In *Genesis* 48:15-19, we read:

"And Jacob blessed Joseph, and said, God, before whom my fathers Abraham and Isaac did walk, the God which fed me all my life long unto this day. The Angel which

redeemed me from all evil, bless the lads; and let my name be named on them [the name of Israel], *and the name of my fathers Abraham and Isaac; and let them grow into a multitude in the midst of the earth. And when Joseph saw that his father laid his right hand upon the head of Ephraim, it displeased him: and he held up his father's hand, to remove it from Ephraim's head unto Manasseh's head. And Joseph said unto his father, Not so, my father: for this is the first-born; put thy right hand upon his head. And his father refused, and said, I know it, my son, I know it: he also* [Manasseh] *shall become a people, and he also shall be great; but truly his younger brother shall be greater than he, and his seed shall become a multitude of nations."*

You will see from these verses that Ephraim, the younger of the two sons of Joseph, was preferred before the elder, Manasseh, and that Jacob said, "Let my name be upon them," the name of Israel. Thus to Ephraim was given the birthright to God's promises to Abraham, including the five-fold promise— the everlasting covenant, the land of Canaan, the multitude of seed, to be the father of many nations, and a source of blessing to the world. Ephraim, as the first-born, had supremacy over the other tribes of Israel.

Now, as we have already seen, the British race is the one in which God is apparently fulfilling His prophecies concerning Israel.

There are many other remarkable identifications between Israel and Great Britain, far more than we have yet been able to refer to. Our churches and cathedrals originally possessed a "Right of sanctuary," carrying out the idea of the cities of refuge, which formed so important a part of the constitution of Israel. We have the law of primogeniture, closely resembling the law given in *Deuteronomy* 21:17; the law of the tithe closely resembling *Leviticus* 27:30; the statute of limitations, which is very much like *Exodus* 21; our land is divided into hundreds and tithings, closely resembling that which you find in *Exodus*

18:21; our weights and measures are of Israelitish descent,[4] and their ten commandments are our ten commandments.

The creation of county councils and district councils is but a return to the Levitical custom of administering the provincial and rural affairs by local authorities, which you will find mentioned in *Isaiah* 1:26. From the legal point of view, it is interesting to notice that our custom of judges going on circuit is exactly what existed in the time of Israel. As we read in I *Samuel* 7:16:

> *"And Samuel went from year to year in circuit to Bethel, and Gilgal, and Mizpeh, and judged Israel in all those places."*

MANASSEH AND THE U.S.A.

While Ephraim was to be the greater, Manasseh also was to become a people and to be called great. Where is Manasseh to-day? Who are the descendants of Manasseh? In *Isaiah* 49:20, we find these words:

> *"The children which thou shalt have, after thou hast lost the other, shall say again in thine ears, The place is too strait for me: give place to me that I may dwell."*

The descendants of Manasseh must be a great people, second only to the descendants of Ephraim. Manasseh was practically the thirteenth tribe of Israel, for Joseph was divided into two, Ephraim and Manasseh. Counting Joseph, there were twelve tribes of Israel; but with Joseph's two sons, who separated into two different tribes, there were thirteen tribes and of these Manasseh was the thirteenth. It is thought by many students of God's Word that in the United States of America we shall find the Manasseh of to-day, and this is the evidence upon which they rely. *Genesis* 48:19 suggests that Manasseh was to

---

[4] *Handbook to the Bible*, pp. 61, 62, Conder (10th Edition).

have a separate destiny, and to become a separate people. It is also clear from this passage that Joseph's two sons will become contemporary nations, the one greater than the other, but both heirs of the blessings promised to Abraham, to Jacob, and to Jacob's seed.

Many students of Scripture also believe that in the United States of America we find the branch of Joseph that was to run over the wall, which is mentioned in *Genesis* 49:22. Manasseh was the thirteenth tribe of Israel, and the number thirteen plays a very important part in much that pertains to the United States of America. In the first place, the original flag of the United States in the year 1777 represents the thirteen original states by thirteen stripes. Again, thirteen letters make up the United States national motto, "E Pluribus Unum," which means "One of a Number." The great seal of the United States on the obverse side has an eagle and olive branch, thirteen arrows and thirteen stars; on the reverse it has the words "Annuit cœptis," which means "He has prospered our undertakings." The United States dollar contains thirteen stars and thirteen letters on the scroll. The eagle on the other side holds thirteen wing feathers, thirteen tail feathers, thirteen arrow heads, thirteen horizontal stripes, and thirteen parallel lines. The original white population of the United States came from England. The Pilgrim Fathers sailed to America, guided by God, as they believed, to find over the seas a land where they could worship in simplicity and in peace. They may well be taken to be the branch which went over the wall.

ISAAC'S SONS

Let me return to one or two more general identifications. Lost Israel when found was to speak another tongue, and not Hebrew (*Isaiah* 28:11). There are many traces of the Hebrew language in our English tongue, and Tyndale, in the preface to his translation of the Bible, says:

"The properties of the Hebrew Tongue agree a thousand times more with the English than with the Latin."

The word "British" is derived from two Hebrew words which mean "Covenant man." The English language is fast becoming the world's vernacular.

Israel's seed is to be called after Isaac—not only after Jacob, but after Isaac. "For in Isaac shall thy seed be called" (*Genesis* 21:12). That is a very important Scriptural statement, so important that it is repeated by Paul in *Romans* 9:7, and is again quoted by the author of the epistle to the *Hebrews* in chapter 11:18: "In Isaac shall thy seed be called." We belong to the Anglo-Saxon race. What is the meaning of this word "Saxon"? The word Saxon undoubtedly means Isaac's Son or the Son of Isaac.

HOW TO SPREAD THE NEWS

Let me call your attention to the text with which I began—*Jeremiah* 31:9—because it tells us how Israel is to be brought back to the knowledge of the Lord.

> *"They shall come with weeping, and with supplications will I lead them: I will cause them to walk by the rivers of waters in a straight way, wherein they shall not stumble; for I am a father to Israel, and Ephraim is my firstborn."*

When God is about to fulfil a prophecy He sets His people praying about it, and creates a spirit of enquiry. This spirit of enquiry concerning the lost tribes of Israel has been created by God among very many of His people.

But how are they to be found? By weepings and by supplications God will lead them; in other words, by united prayer. Only God can teach men concerning His will. Not by human argument, not by human rhetoric: but by the Word of God and the Spirit of God. So I am very hopeful that God will use the prayers of His people to bring to light His truth in an abundant and wonderful degree, helping them to proclaim to an astonished world the kingdom of Israel.

Let us never forget that, however interesting the prophetic study may be, however grand the prophetic outlook may appear, however wonderful the fact that the fulfilment of these promises has been carried on through the centuries—to be discovered in this last century—let us never forget that if we are to understand the prophecies aright we must ourselves be right with God, and that unless we are filled with the Holy Ghost our knowledge of prophecy will be futile, and our historical knowledge useless.

May God teach us how to pray, and so bless us individually that we shall have the light of His countenance upon the Word of His truth, and being right with Him ourselves we shall be able to convey the truth to others.

CHAPTER V

ISRAEL'S WANDERINGS

GENEALOGY, KING DAVID TO KING EDWARD

HEBREW AND BRITISH EMBLEMS

THE STONE OF DESTINY

We will now study our subject with regard to the following: (1) Israel's wanderings from Media to Britain; (2) The genealogy from King David to King Edward the Seventh; (3) The Hebrew and the British emblems; (4) The Stone of Destiny—from Bethel to Westminster Abbey.

(1). Let us trace Israel's wanderings from Media to Britain. It is an historical fact that within about a hundred years of the commencement of their captivity the ten tribes escaped from Media. The Jewish historian Esdras, in his second book in the Apocrypha, says:

"The ten tribes took this counsel among themselves, that they should leave the multitude of the heathen and go forth into a further country, that there they might keep their law, which they had never kept in their own land, and they passed by the way of the Euphrates."

Probably there was revolution in Media at the time, and the captives took the opportunity of escaping. Josephus, the historian, writing AD 70, confirms this by saying:

"The ten tribes are now beyond the Euphrates, and are an immense multitude."

What became of them? The ten tribes were undoubtedly known to the ancient Greeks and Romans under various names. Sometimes they were called the Goths, sometimes the Scythians, sometimes the Sakai, and it is an undoubted fact that a large number of them occupied the shores of the Black Sea. Herodotus, Pliny, and Ptolemy, all refer to them as having come from Media across the Euphrates.

John Milton, in his history of Britain, says of the Saxons:

> "They were a people thought by good writers to be descended from the Scythians or Sakai, afterwards called Sacasons, who with a flood of other nations came into Europe about the time of the decline of the Roman Empire."

In a recent book called *The Viking Age* written by M. du Chaillu, it has been asserted that the ancestors of the English came from the shores of the Black Sea. It is no doubt true that at the present time there are old grave-stones in the Crimea, on the banks of the Black Sea, which are clearly of Israelitish origin. One of these grave-stones still retains the following inscription:

> "Zadok the Levite, son of Moses, died 4,000 years after creation, 785 years after our exile."

A town on the Danube near the Black Sea is to-day called Isakcha, evidently an Israelitish name, while another town bears a name similar to that of Joseph's wife.

It seems therefore that the ten tribes, or a large proportion of them, moved from Media to the shores of the Black Sea, about the commencement of the Christian era, where they remained for centuries. From thence they moved northwards, and some went into Scandinavia and others to Western Europe. The people whom we call Saxons were not natives of England, but captured it from the ancient Britons, and had themselves come from the shores of the Black Sea.

On arrival in England the Saxons divided the country into various sections, of which many were called after their own name, and which names we use to-day. For instance, Sussex meant South Saxon; Essex, East Saxon; Wessex, West Saxon; Middlesex, Middle Saxon. The word "Saxon" is traced to "Sac's sons," or sons of Isaac, and is claimed to be a fulfilment of *Genesis* 21:12, where we have the prophecy:

"In Isaac shall thy seed be called."

The Normans, who conquered the Saxons in the eleventh century, were not Frenchmen, but Northmen, people from Scandinavia, to whom a hundred years before the French king had ceded a portion of his dominions, which was called after them, namely, Normandy. These Northmen are believed to be part of the tribe of Benjamin. They were very remarkable people. Lord Macaulay says:

"The Northmen were the foremost race of Christendom. Their valour, their ferocity, made them conspicuous from the Black Sea to the Atlantic Ocean."

They are believed to be descended from Benjamin because of their character, which was the character of that tribe, and also because the Norman standard was a wolf, which also was the standard of the tribe of Benjamin.

"Benjamin shall ravin as a wolf" (*Genesis* 49:27).

What the British race has accomplished since the Norman Conquest is a matter of history, and in my third chapter we saw that Great Britain fulfils in a very remarkable degree the prophecies concerning Israel.

"*Great* Britain!" A strange name for a few small islands at the far-Western point of Europe! Why were they called Great Britain? It sounds almost absurd when you come to think of it. There must be some reason for it. Is it because this country has been the home for these many centuries of the greatest nation that the world has seen or ever will see?

Much of what I have said rests upon tradition, but tradition is the basis of history, and if we turn from tradition as untrue we shall lose an important source of knowledge.

KING DAVID TO KING EDWARD

(2). The genealogy from King David to King Edward the Seventh. While the birthright was Ephraim's, Judah was to rule. David said:

> "*The Lord God ... chose me ... to be king over Israel for ever: for he hath chosen Judah to be the ruler*" (I *Chronicles* 28:4).

And Jeremiah, writing four hundred years later, said:

> "*For thus saith the Lord: David shall never want a man to sit upon the throne of the house of Israel*" (*Jeremiah* 33:17).

We may expect therefore to find that the King of England is in direct descent from the Kings of Judah. King Edward the Seventh's ancestry is traced back through James the First of England and the Sixth of Scotland to Kenneth MacAlpin, who was the first king of Scotland, AD 834; through him to Feargus More, the King of Argyllshire, AD 487; and through him to the kings of Ireland, right back through fifty-four kings to the year 580 BC.

Tradition says that about that time King Heremon married an Eastern princess, whose name was Tea Tephi, and who was, according to Irish legend, the daughter of Zedekiah, the last king of Judah. King Zedekiah's eyes were put out by the Chaldeans; his sons were destroyed, but, as you will see in *Jeremiah* 43:6, his daughters escaped.

One of those daughters says the legend, escaped to Ireland and became the bride of the Irish king. (You must remember that the tribe of Dan had long possessed ships and navigated the Mediterranean, and were not unacquainted with the shores of Spain and of Britain.) This daughter of Zedekiah was apparently entrusted by God to the care of the prophet Jeremiah. If you will turn to *Jeremiah* 1:10, you will see these words addressed to the prophet:

> *"I have this day set thee over the nations and over the kingdoms, to root out, and to pull down, and to destroy, and to throw down, to build, and to plant."*

Then look at II *Kings* 19:30, 31:

> *"And the remnant that is escaped of the house of Judah shall yet again take root downward, and bear fruit upward: For out of Jerusalem shall go forth a remnant, and they that escape out of Mount Zion. The zeal of the Lord of Hosts shall do this."*

It was evidently the Divine intention that a remnant of the tribe of Judah should escape and "bear fruit" elsewhere; and so we are not surprised to learn that, according to Irish legend, about the year 580 BC—that is to say, about the date of the captivity of Judah—a princess from the East arrived in the North of Ireland. She was accompanied by two people, one of whom was described as her guardian and declared to have been a prophet, and another was named Brug. If you read *Jeremiah* 43:6, you will see the account of the escape and who this was:

> *"Men and women and children, and the king's daughters, and every person that Nebuzaradan the captain of the guard had left with Gedaliah the son of Ahikam, the son of Shaphan, and Jeremiah the prophet, and Baruch the son of Neriah."*

Irish legend therefore says that an oriental princess arrived about this time in Ireland, accompanied by a prophet and by another man from the East. It is also no doubt true that from that time many new things were introduced into Ireland. We find that Tara, a Hebrew word, means "The law of the two tables." We find the school of the prophets introduced into Ireland. False worship, the worship of Baal, was put an end to, and the worship of the true God instituted, all within the next hundred years.

If then these legends are to be believed, and if early Irish history is correct, from this Eastern princess there sprang a line of ancestry to Fergus, king of Ireland, who afterwards became king of Argyllshire, and whose descendants became kings of Scotland, and so on down to our present Queen Elizabeth II.

It is said—and I do not think it is any secret—that the Royal Family of England are deeply interested in this subject. When you remember how many European thrones have tottered in the past, well may they believe in these prophecies, and rest their hope in the Word of God. There is no doubt that the late Queen Victoria was herself interested in this, and it is said that she showed the Rev. Mr. Glover, who was a great authority on this subject, her own genealogy right back to King David. The eldest son of the present King has, among other names, that of David, by which he is known in the Royal Family circle. By the year AD 1924 Prince David will be thirty years of age, and when he reaches his thirtieth year one hundred generations of thirty years each will have been completed since David was anointed king of Israel.[5]

EMBLEMS

(3). We will look into the Hebrew and British emblems. The British national heraldry corresponds in a remarkable way to the heraldry of Israel. The national emblems of Great Britain are the Lion and the Unicorn. Now the Lion was the emblem of the tribe of Judah which carried the Royal Line of Israel through King David.

STONE OF DESTINY

(4). In conclusion, let us study the history of the Stone of Destiny. On this subject there can be very little left to conjecture, for this Stone—a most wonderful national

---

[5] By 2014 there will have been one hundred and three generations of thirty years each (12th Edition).

emblem—is now part of the Coronation Chair in Westminster Abbey[6], and every British king or queen except Queen Mary, from Edward the First to Edward the Seventh has been crowned upon it. Queen Mary, being Roman Catholic, had a Coronation Chair of her own, which she sent over to Rome to be blessed by the Pope,

Every other English monarch, from Edward the First to Edward the Seventh, has been crowned upon that Stone. It is a rough oblong stone, 22 inches long, 13 inches broad, and 11 inches deep, with veins of red and white running through it, which was brought from Scotland to this country by Edward the First, and has been used as the Coronation Stone for 600 years in this country. When Edward the Seventh was anointed king the sacred oil was poured upon him on that Stone, exactly as the oil was poured upon King David thousands of years before. For 800 years before it was brought to England it was the Coronation Stone of Scotland; and before that it came from Ireland, where fifty-four kings of Ireland had been crowned upon it. Well might Dean Stanley say that of all national emblems, and of all our national treasures, this Stone of Destiny, which has always been called Jacob's Stone, is probably the most wonderful that this country possesses. Now read *Genesis* 28:10:

> *"And Jacob went out from Beer-sheba, and went toward Haran. And he lighted upon a certain place, and tarried there all night, because the sun was set: and he took of the stones of that place and put them for his pillows, and lay down in that place to sleep. And he dreamed, and behold a ladder set up on the earth, and the top of it reached to heaven: and behold, the angels of God ascending and descending on it. And, behold, the Lord stood above it, and said, I am the Lord God of Abraham thy father, and the God of Isaac: the land whereon thou liest, to thee will I give it, and to thy seed; And thy seed shall be as the dust of the earth; and thou shalt spread abroad to the west, and to the east, and to the north, and to the south; and*

---

[6] In 1996 the Coronation Stone was removed to Scotland where it is on display in Edinburgh Castle (12th Edition).

in thee and in thy seed shall all the families of the earth be blessed. And, behold, I am with thee, and will keep thee in all places whither thou goest, and will bring thee again into this land; for I will not leave thee, until I have done that which I have spoken to thee of. And Jacob awaked out of his sleep, and he said, Surely the Lord is in this place, and I knew it not. And he was afraid, and said, How dreadful is this place! This is none other but the house of God, and this is the gate of heaven. And Jacob rose up early in the morning, and took the stone that he had put for his pillows, and set it up for a pillar, and poured oil upon the top of it."

There is a tradition that the Stone which now rests in Westminster Abbey is the same stone as that upon which Jacob rested his head. It is believed—and there is a good deal of Scripture to support their belief—that on his return Jacob took this stone with him as a token of the Divine Presence, and on his deathbed made reference to it in relation to Joseph and his descendants. In *Genesis* 49:24, you will find that Jacob, in blessing Joseph, refers to:

"The stone of Israel."

Perhaps the meaning of the passage is that Joseph's sons were to take charge of the stone, which would be to them a symbol of the Shepherd of Israel. But some Hebrew scholars give us the literal meaning of these words: "Henceforth he (Joseph) takes care of this stone of Israel." Evidently a stone or piece of rock was brought out of Egypt by the Israelites at the time of the Exodus when Joseph's bones were carried by them out of Egypt; and this may have been what Paul referred to in I *Corinthians* 10:4:

"The Rock that followed them."

Not the rock that led them, but the rock that followed them. Perhaps this very stone was the one which Moses struck, for "the rock that followed them" must have been a moving rock. When Christ came He compared Himself to a stone which the builders rejected but which was become the corner stone or head-stone of the building. The Jews also believed that Jacobs's stone formed part of Solomon's temple.

The Irish legend goes on to say that when Jeremiah escaped with Zedekiah's daughter, accompanied by Brug, and came by means of the boats of Dan first to Spain—where, according to the legend, they were wrecked—and then from Spain to Ireland, they brought this stone with them, and that from that time it became the crowning-stone of the Irish kings. After this, as I have told you, it became the crowning-stone of the Kings of Argyll, and then of the Kings of Scotland, and now is the crowning-stone of the Kings of England.

One thing is certain—that we have in Westminster Abbey a very remarkable Stone, associated with the British monarchy, the origin of which no one can explain apart from these ancient traditions. Sir Walter Scott wrote of this stone:

> "Unless the fates have faithless grown,
> And prophet's voice be vain,
> Where'er is found this sacred stone,
> The wanderers' race will reign."

These words have certainly proved true. Wherever that stone has been, the wanderers' race has reigned in Ireland, in Scotland, in England. Geologists say—and Canon Tristram in his book quotes what they say—that this Stone could not possibly have come originally from Ireland. No similar rock has ever been discovered in Ireland, but rocks of a similar type are to be found in Palestine.

The objection may again be raised that this is all very wonderful but that it rests to a large extent upon tradition. Tradition, however, is the earlier basis of all history. This is more than tradition; it has thousands of years of historical basis. The tradition is that which goes beyond the history and tells us that which strangely coincides with the prophecies and the history of the Bible. These remarkable identifications concerning the people of Israel and the Anglo-Saxon race are, like all God's truth, more difficult to disbelieve than to believe.

It may be asked, "What possible good will come to us from troubling as to whether the British race contains the descendants of the ten tribes?" I will deal with this question in my closing pages, now merely saying this: Let the British people become convinced that they are the descendants of the ten tribes, and it will put the question of our national precedence in a light which we have never yet known and will probably give an impetus to Bible study that we have never yet seen. It will prove God's Word literally true in a wonderful measure. The most eminent unbelievers of the past 150 years have gone out of their way to declare that they were unbelievers because they were asked to believe in the spiritual interpretation of the promises of God, though they were told that the wonderful promises about Israel had either not been literally fulfilled or could not be accepted. I believe that the acceptance of the literal truth of God's promises concerning Israel will immensely help every one of us in our faith in the fulfilment of the spiritual promises of God.

CHAPTER VI

OF WHAT VALUE IS THIS TRUTH?

Now let us deal, in conclusion, with some of the main objections which have been raised, and generally answer the question: "Of what value is this truth?"

The first objection which I have received is this: "Is not the British-Israel Truth contrary to the scheme of Christianity, which admits all nations and favours none?"

It is not contrary to the scheme of Christianity that one nation should have special advantages, for it has been God's method from the beginning. God originally chose Israel by covenant, and in *Deuteronomy* 7:6, He gives the reason:

> *"For thou art an holy people unto the Lord thy God: the Lord thy God hath chosen thee to be a special people unto himself, above all people that are upon the face of the earth. The Lord did not set his love upon you, nor choose you, because ye were more in number than any people: for ye were the fewest of all people; But because the Lord loved you, and because he would keep the oath which he had sworn unto your fathers, hath the Lord brought you out with a mighty hand, and redeemed you out of the house of bondmen, from the hand of Pharaoh, king of Egypt."*

The separate existence of the house of Israel in New Testament times was recognised by the Lord Jesus Christ. He spoke of

> *"The lost sheep of the House of Israel."*

He could not have been referring to the Jews, because the Jews were not lost but were all around Him, and in their own land. Christ must have referred in this passage to the ten tribes, who for more than 700 years had been wanderers among the nations, and He went on to say that to restore Israel—to restore the ten tribes to communion with God—was part of the great mission of Himself and of His disciples. When He gave His commission to the apostles He said:

> *"Go not in the way of the Gentiles, and into any city of the Samaritans enter ye not, but go rather to the lost sheep of the House of Israel."*

We may therefore safely say that this subject is not contrary to Christianity, but was evidently in our Lord's mind and referred to by Him.

DESPISE NOT THE BIRTHRIGHT

The next objection is: "Are we not just as well off whether we are Abraham's seed or not, because as Christ is the Saviour of all men, He is necessarily the Saviour of the British race?"

No, we are not, because there are both present and future advantages connected with being the Israel of God. Christ Himself declared that some particular nation was ordained to receive the Gospel on its rejection by the Jews. He said in *Matthew* 21:43:

> *"The Kingdom of God shall be taken from you* [that is to say, from the Jews] *and given to a nation bringing forth the fruits thereof."*

It is a significant fact that before the overthrow of Jerusalem in AD 70 by the Romans, and within thirty years of the Crucifixion, Christianity had already been received into Britain, from which time until the present the British have been, at least nominally, a Christian people. We see here the Divine plan of Israel's priority among the nations. The kingdom rejected by Judah was given to Israel, the other branch of the seed of Abraham, to whom it belonged by covenant. So there is plainly a distinct advantage in being of the seed of Abraham.

Let me remind you that for centuries Britain has been happy, free, in a measure godly, and in the forefront of earth's civilisation, while other nations have continued in comparative ignorance and barbarism. Ours, therefore, is the privilege of being the first nation to drink of the cup of salvation, the first nation to hand it on to other races and thus to fulfil the promises made to Abraham, that his seed should be blessed to all nations. Well may we say:

"The Lord hath done great things for us, whereof we are glad" (*Psalm* 126:2).

"O Israel, who is like unto thee, O people saved by the Lord" (*Deuteronomy* 33:29).

CIRCUMCISION

Another difficulty raised by many is that if we belonged to the lost tribes we should possess the rite of circumcision.

My answer is that Israel abandoned the Mosaic ritual, with its circumcision, and substituted the religion and ceremonies of Baal 200 years before they went into captivity. Let us also remember that with the introduction of Christianity the law of circumcision was abolished, and that the ten tribes did not return to God until the Gospel era had begun, and that therefore the law of circumcision was no longer applicable to them.

Still another objection is: "The British nation consists of many mixed nationalities: how can they all be Israel?"

Israel came to these Islands at different times, by different routes, and in different bands—Angles, Saxons, Jutes, Danes, and Normans.

Someone else writes: "If we are Israel we must all return to Palestine, and there will not be room for us."

The future occupation of Palestine by Israel and Judah will be representative. *Jeremiah* 3:14, says:

> *"Turn, O backsliding children, saith the Lord; ... take you one of a city, and two of a family, and I will bring you to Zion."*

All Israel will not necessarily go back to Palestine, but will hold Palestine, probably, very much as the British nation holds India to-day—representatively. Let us also remember that Abraham's covenant gives to his seed not only Palestine but a very much larger tract of country, and afterwards declares that Abraham and his seed are heirs of the whole world.

The next objection is: "Is not Britain great and glorious because she is Christian and not because she is Israel?" Britain's Christian privileges and opportunities have been great, but her measuring up to her privileges has been lacking. There are other peoples who have been better Christians than we have been. The Moravians 150 years ago put to shame every other form of Christianity in the world; they were so eager to spread the knowledge of Jesus Christ that they actually sold themselves into slavery to win the heathen.

SEEK THE TRUE MEANING

The next question is: "Will it not suffice to claim the spiritual meaning of the promises made to Israel?"

No, it will not, and when we realise the literal promise and claim, and do our part to bring about the fulfilment, we will enjoy the spiritual meaning of it better. How can we accept the spiritual meanings to God's promises and ignore their plain literal meaning? Let me tell you what Dr Ryle, the late Bishop of Liverpool, said:

> "I warn you that unless you interpret the prophetical portion of the Old Testament in the simple, literal meaning

of its words, you will find it no easy matter to carry on an argument with an intelligent Jew. Will you dare to tell him that Zion, Jerusalem, Jacob, Judah, Ephraim, Israel, did not mean what they seem to mean, but mean the Church of Christ? I believe it is high time for the Church of Christ to awake out of its sleep about Old Testament prophecy. From the time of the Old Fathers down to the present day men have gone on in a pernicious habit of spiritualising the words of the prophets until their true meaning has been well-nigh buried."

The Bishop goes on to say:

"For centuries there has prevailed in the Churches of Christ an unwarrantable mode of dealing with the word 'Israel.' It has been interpreted in many passages of the Psalms and Prophets as if it meant nothing more than Christian believers. Have promises been held out to Israel? Men have been told continually that they are addressed to Gentile saints. Have glorious things been described as laid up in store for Israel? Men have been insistently told that they described the victories and triumphs of the gospel in Christian Churches."

The Bishop then adds:

"In reading the words which God addressed to His ancient people never lose sight of the primary sense of the text."

The question, "Will it not suffice to claim the spiritual meaning of the promises?" is therefore answered by my saying: No, I think we are able to claim the spiritual meaning a great deal better when we pay God the compliment of believing His words in their literal sense as well as in their spiritual.

WHAT'S THE GOOD OF IT?

I come now to the main question, which so many have asked: "What is the good of this teaching?"

How can men dare to ask such a question regarding that which occupies so large a part of Scripture and which, as God Himself declares in *Jeremiah* 32:41, occupies His whole heart and soul? I will, however, endeavour to answer this question.

"Granting that the British-Israel Truth is correct, what advantage may result?"

In the first place, it proves the truth and inspiration of the Scriptures and creates an intelligent and earnest interest in their study, to the destruction of that veiled scepticism or indifference so common among all denominations today.

In the second place, we will find it is a master key to the Old Testament and to much of the New. I believe that under the light and power of the Holy Ghost it unlocks the truth, clearing away mysteries and explaining passages which have hitherto been riddles. Take, for example, in the 37th chapter of *Ezekiel*, the vision of the dry bones, which is familiar to all of us. Christian teachers constantly spiritualise this passage, and make this vision of the dry bones to mean the conversion of sinners, in spite of the fact that God says in the 11th verse:

"Son of man, these bones are the whole house of Israel: behold, they say, Our bones are dried, and our hope is lost: we are cut off for our parts. Therefore prophesy and say unto them, Thus saith the Lord God: Behold, O my people, I will open your graves, and cause you to come up out of your graves, and bring you into the land of Israel. And ye shall know that I am the Lord, when I have opened your graves, O my people, and brought you up out of your graves. And shall put my Spirit in you, and ye shall live; and I shall place you in your own land; then shall ye know that I the Lord have spoken it, and performed it, saith the Lord."

It is impossible in the face of these words *only* to spiritualise such a passage as this. If we use this passage in preaching to sinners, we will do well to declare its real literal meaning, and then show them that over and above the literal meaning there is also the spiritual meaning.

SOULS AND BODIES

Thirdly. It makes men associate God with the material as well as with the spiritual, just as our Lord did when He said to the Jews concerning the sick of the palsy:

> *"Whether is easier to say . . . Thy sins are forgiven; or to say, Arise, and take up thy bed and walk? But that ye may know that the Son of man hath power on earth to forgive sins (he saith to the sick of the palsy), I say unto thee, Arise, take up thy bed, and go to thy house. And he arose . . ."* (*Mark* 2:9-12, R.V.).

We are very apt to dissociate the Almighty God from His material universe. God is the God of the material universe as much as He is of the spiritual universe. He regards our bodies as well as our souls, our homes as well as our churches, our business as well as our Christian work.

Fourthly. It gives a new basis for the exercise of faith even with regard to Old Testament passages which we have interpreted spiritually in the past. Take, for instance, the 36th chapter of *Ezekiel*, familiar to every member of the Pentecostal League. We have used it again and again, and seen wonderful results; but if read in the light of this truth it will appear much stronger than ever before, especially if we finish with the 37th verse, which says:

> *"I will yet for this be enquired of by the house of Israel, to do it for them."*

If we take our place in the House of Israel, we can pray for the fulfilment of these promises in a way we never did before.

WHAT BRADLAUGH SAID

Fifthly. It will to a large extent silence the infidel. If we take the three foremost infidels of modern times—Tom Paine, David Hume and Charles Bradlaugh—we find that all three in large measure base their infidelity on the apparent failure or non-fulfilment of the Bible promise to Israel. I knew Charles Bradlaugh, and I can quote what he said upon this subject. Charles Bradlaugh said this:

"God a God of truth! Why, He promised to Abraham in the most solemn words, He repeated His promise, and He has not kept His word. This Bible which reveals the attributes of Almighty God, tells us that God condescended to swear to a puny man that He would establish his kingdom for ever, and that his seed should be as numerous as the sand upon the seashore. That promise was reiterated and sworn to by God, and I ask, where is that kingdom now? Here? Do not tell me that it is meant figuratively; do not tell me that it is not literal. God swore that it should be for ever. He establishes it, and now it is a thing of the past, and you tell me that the God of the Bible always speaks the truth. I do not believe it."

This is a terrible impeachment, and indeed unanswerable unless we accept this truth which destroys this impeachment, proves the Bible true, and silences the infidel; nay, it will do more than that, for it will be likely to attract, arouse, arrest and win him for God.

"He which converteth the sinner from the error of his way shall save a soul from death, and shall hide a multitude of sins" (*James* 5:20).

Sixthly. The acceptance of this truth by the Christians of today would, I believe, lead to an immediate revival among all sections of the British race. In the first place, it would attract and arouse the attention of men to the subject of the Christian religion. Missionary work among the nations would be revived. Britain herself would awake to her national responsibilities as the chosen people of God, His ordained instrument in carrying out His purposes in the world. I think it will lead to the conversion of the Jews. The veil would be taken away; the brotherhood of the British and Jewish people would be established, and thus Israel would be saved.

Lastly. I think it would hasten the return of our Lord and the millennial dispensation. It would provide the Lord with a Throne, a People, and a country. Much more even than this would be the result of acceptance of this truth. May the Spirit of God guide and direct those to whom I speak in these pages!

It is especially interesting to me—who began this inquiry with a desire simply to know the truth, and who now closes it convinced that this is the truth—to know that so many thousands of earnest, ardent, holy men and women are having their attention called to this most important subject. Many earnest believers who have been out and out for God on spiritual truth will now be led to consider and study and pray over the literal meaning of these passages.

FOR US AND FOR OTHERS

Let us not, like Esau, despise our birthright. We have often boasted that we believe the Bible from cover to cover, but so long as we ignore its literal promises concerning the people of God we fail to do so. The truth of God can never harm us. This truth disappoints no hopes, imperils no interests, damages no institutions, but is good tidings of great joy to all people.

The supremacy of the British race is not due to any inherent good in us, but to the sovereign gift of God Who saves us. Let us, therefore, cry, "Not unto us, O Lord, not unto us, but unto Thy name be the glory, for Thy mercy and for Thy truth's sake," and, humbly bowing before our God, claim the Spirit of God to take of the things of Jesus Christ, and show us His will, His purpose, His plan; His desire for us, for our nation, for other nations through us, and for the Church of Christ in all its branches.

FURTHER READING

The Stone of Destiny by F. Wallace Connon

Daughters of Destiny by Glyn S. Lewis

Why does Britain have the Lion and the Unicorn?
by F. Wallace Connon

The Post-Captivity Names of Israel
by Rev. W. Pascoe Goard

The Names of God by Rev. W. Pascoe Goard

All books from Covenant Publishing

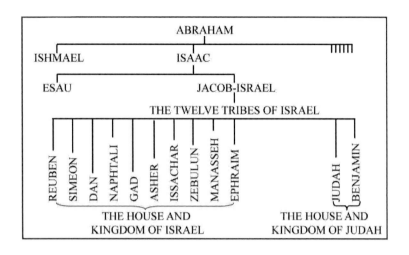

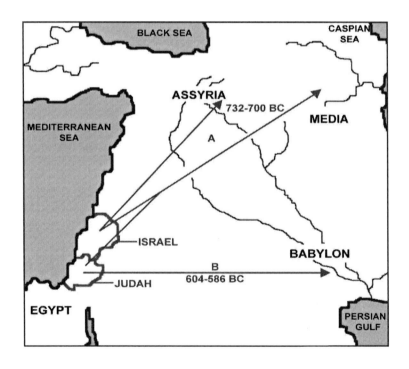

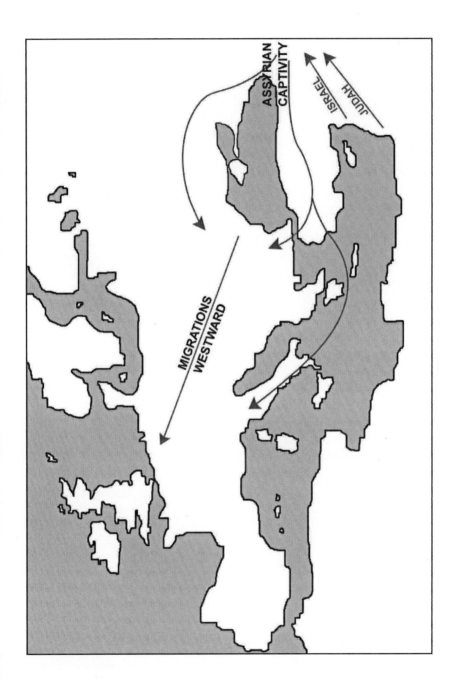